WISDOM NUGGETS
FOR EVERYDAY LIFE

KNOWLEDGE IS A POWERFUL TOOL, BUT KNOWLEDGE
WITHOUT WISDOM IS MERE THEORY WITHOUT INTELLIGENCE.

NANA-SEI TWERETWIE

WISDOM NUGGETS FOR EVERYDAY LIFE

©2024 Rev.Nana-Sei Tweretwie

All rights reserved, No part of this publication may be reproduced, stored in a retieval system, or transmitted, in any form, or by any means(electronic, mechanical, photocopying, recording or otherwise) without the prior written permission of the publisher.

Published by: Rev Nana-Sei Tweretwie
Scriptural references are from;
The King James Version
The New King James Version
American Standard Version
Easy-To-Read Version (ERV)
English Standard Version
Lexham English Bible
New Living Translation
New Revised Standard Version
New International Version
The New Cambridge Paragraph
Bible with the Apocrypha

Acknowledgements

My deepest gratitude goes to:

1. God the Father, Our Lord Jesus Christ, and the Holy Spirit who has made me who I am today. There is no way I can come this far without His mercies and grace.

2. My wife, Rev. Mrs. Yvonne Tweretwie and children for their love and great support.

3. My spiritual children, Josephine Osei and Comfort Adusei, who contributed immensely to this glorious work.

4. Amenyo Kwame Akoto for your encouragement and support and all the friends and families.

5. Rev. Dr. Glenn M. Balfour, Theologian in Residence, Assemblies of God Great Britain, who assisted me in my pursuit of an MA in Biblical Studies. Studying for a Masters degree with a minimal formal education is not an easy task, and Rev Dr Glenn's assistance was invaluable.

6. Rev. Prof. Nana Kyei-Baffour, Healthcare Chaplain, Course Director of Postgraduate Education in Healthcare Chaplaincy, Adjunct Professor with Global University (Assemblies of God, USA) and Senior Pastor at Victory-City Assemblies of God, Wallington-London. Rev. Prof. Nana Kyei-Baffour is an outstanding person who is willing to go the extra mile to point me in the right direction. May the Lord Almighty bless you for being there for me.

7. Rev. Dr. Samuel Boateng, through whom the calling of God upon my life became clear. Reverend, God bless you and your family for everything you have done for me.

8. Mr. Baizy, the man who taught me how to communicate in English, may the Lord remember you in due time. I really appreciate you, Sir.

Dedication

I dedicate this book to the glory of God, whose grace and wisdom have guided every word written within these pages. To Jesus Christ, the source of all wisdom, knowledge and truth, whose love and sacrifice have been the foundation of my faith and inspiration. I also dedicate this work to the Holy Spirit, who has given me strength, in-depth understanding, many revelations, and the power to accomplish this glorious work. Again, to those seeking a deeper relationship with the Lord, especially the Body of Christ, and those who are ordained for eternal life yet have not received the Lord. I pray that these words of wisdom lead you closer to the Lord and fill your life with His unending peace, joy and wisdom to fulfil His divine purpose in life. May this book serve as a beacon of hope and light for all who read it, in Jesus Mighty Name. Amen!

Foreword

Reverend Nana-Sei Tweretwie has an established Pentecostal Ministry and experience that makes him eminently suited to write Wisdom Nuggets for Everyday Life. Having ministered fruitfully and faithfully in church leadership contexts in both Ghana and the United Kingdom, he has the ability to bring scripture to life in a manner that transcends a single cultural lens. His academic training coupled with his ministry and church leadership experience enables him to bring considered thinking into a genuinely inspirational setting.

One result of these remarkable combinations is this publication. In it, he brings spiritual insight, theological observation, and biblical erudition to bear on thirty aspects of everyday life. Each short chapter is thoroughly accessible, genuinely informed, and has the potential to enrich and inspire the reader.

This publication would work wonderfully as a month's devotional reading plan, a study guide for small groups in a church's annual cycle, or even a table-top resource for the reader to delve into as and when. However it is used, it is sure to live up to its title and offer nuggets of wisdom designed to inspire and even transform everyday life.

Rev. Dr. Glenn Balfour,
Theologian-in-Residence, Assemblies of God GB

Contents

Acknowledgements iii
Dedication v
Foreword vi
Introduction 1
1. Self-Discovery 3
2. Be Yourself 7
3. Know Yourself 13
4. Daily Diligence 19
5. At Your Doorstep 23
6. No Laziness 27
7. Be Focused 31
8. Avoid Distractions 36
9. Confidence 40
10. Live in Dignity 43
11. Spiritual Fortitude 47
12. Self-Doubt 51
13. Self-Belief 55
14. Labels 60
15. Consider the Needy 64
16. All Die 67
17. One Life 71
18. Prepare Ahead 75

19. Seek Knowledge 79
20. True Knowledge 83
21. Face Failure 87
22. Born to Win 91
23. You Will Not Fail 95
24. Pursue Mastery 101
25. Yes, You Can 105
26. Resilience 109
27. No Place For Ignorance 113
28. Keep Moving 117
29. Above Your Peers 121
30. Correct Your Mistakes 125
Further Reading and References 129
Bibliography 130
Author's Profile 133

Introduction

Life can be challenging and frustrating, but with the word of God and the guidance of the Holy Spirit, we can navigate the journey and emerge victorious. While there are numerous resources on Christian living, *Wisdom Nuggets for Everyday Life* stands out with its unique approach. This book has been crafted to guide individuals in their daily lives, emphasizing key areas to focus on and providing practical ways to integrate Christian faith into their routines, empowering readers to apply these teachings in their everyday lives.

Wisdom Nuggets for Everyday Life is more than just a book. It's a beacon of motivation and encouragement for those who aspire to be deeply rooted in their faith. This book offers practical and insightful guiding principles to help individuals navigate the challenges of everyday life and maintain a healthy balance between their spiritual and physical journeys. It imparts knowledge and wisdom that can be utilised to enhance one's quality of life by employing biblical principles in real-world scenarios.

Wisdom Nuggets for Everyday Life was inspired by the Lord's prompting to transform my morning walk into a prayer walk.

I was motivated to write over 18 wisdom sayings on the same day that I initiated the devotional walk.

As this book provides you with biblical principles for real-life situations, it is imperative that at the end of every chapter, you take the opportunity to introspect and meditate on the words you have read and ask yourself some practical questions to reflect on and answer as they relate to your life. This makes you self-aware of your life situation and helps you compare your life with the word of God, thereby configuring how to align yourself with the word of God. By reflecting on your beliefs, actions, and thoughts in comparison to the teachings of the Bible, you can identify areas where you may need to make changes or seek guidance. This self-awareness and principles can lead to personal growth, spiritual development, empowerment, and a deeper connection with God. Ultimately, aligning yourself with the word of God can bring you peace, fulfilment, and purpose in your life.

1
Self-Discovery

Only you are you, and you can only be you.
Discover yourself, and you will be a better you.

> "I am fearfully and wonderfully made.
> ……When I was made in secret,
> And skillfully wrought in the lowest parts of the earth."
>
> **Psalm 139:14-15**

God designed everyone to be unique, with their own set of gifts, talents, strengths, and weaknesses. It is vital for each of us to accept our individuality and not try to conform to the expectations of others. We can create a more diverse and inclusive society by acknowledging our differences and recognising the value of every person's uniqueness. Embracing our individuality allows us to fully realise our potential and positively impact the world around us.

Your distinctive and peculiar qualities are not just unique, but they set you apart from others. Your approach to life and your unique perspective are what make you stand out in a crowd. Hold on to these characteristics and let them shine, for they are what make you truly special and one-of-a-kind.

Self-discovery is imperative to ascertaining your true uniqueness. Engage in a moment of introspection regarding your true self and the contribution you can make to the world we all love to live in. Reflect on your love, passions, qualities, and beliefs to uncover the true purpose that your maker has placed you on earth to accomplish. David Benner believes we are *"created from love, of love and for love, our existence makes no sense apart from Divine love."* Without this love, we are lost and incomplete, wandering aimlessly in a world that offers no true relief. Only through the knowledge of divine love can we truly find meaning and purpose in our lives. Therefore, we can be fruitful, multiply, replenish, and subdue the earth as God commanded from the beginning (Genesis 1:28). So, the endowment of His blessing over our lives here in Genesis is the catalyst that enables us to fulfil our destiny.

This blessing of God upon our lives makes anything possible when we discover who we truly are. Glory be to the name of our Lord Jesus Christ, who loved us to the point of death, shed His blood to redeem us from our sins, and constantly reminded us of the endowment blessing of God that makes each of us unique and wonderful. Every person has a God-given talent, and if you discover yours, you will be able to show up in the world as a better version of yourself. As you journey through life, you should always remind yourself that you do not have to yield or conform to societal norms and pressures in order to determine who you are. Only you can truly determine who you are when carrying on your 'own shoulders' all the responsibilities required to make the best version of yourself.

REFLECTIONS

- What one thing do people often say to describe your personality?

2
Be Yourself

Never try to be a better someone; always try to better yourself.

> "... that we also may be like all the nations."
> **1 Samuel 8:20**

We often do not acknowledge the importance of seeking God's love and strength and live in it. This was one of the biggest challenges for the people of Israel (1 Sam 8:20). They had the God of all the earth on their leader and God, the patriarchs, the law, the promise of the Messiah, and the best of the best of the land – yet they had contradictory preferences. What were they seeking? They sought a king who judges and leads them to war like other nations around them (1 Samuel 8:4). And what was God's response? He forewarned them about the consequences of their choices, but they would not listen. They insisted, and so God yielded to their request (1 Samuel 8:4-21).

Their experience brings out some important lessons for us:

Impatience and short-sightedness are a poisonous pill that destroys destiny. It blinds us to the opportunities and lessons to learn in the present moment, causing us to rush ahead and make hasty decisions that can have long-lasting consequences. Therefore, when we allow impatience to take hold of us, we lose sight of the beauty of the journey and the opportunities that come from facing challenges with grace and resilience. If we learn to cultivate patience, we can unlock the full potential of our destiny and enjoy the process of becoming who we are truly meant to be.

Whenever we demean ourselves in comparison to others, we displease God, who made us. Bertrand Russell (1930) firmly believed that *"Envy is one of the fundamental causes of human suffering, and he counselled his readers to avoid it."* Unfortunately, this is still happening today: *"The habit of thinking in terms of comparison is a fatal one ... which consists in seeing things never in themselves but only in their relations. ..."* The constant need to evaluate ourselves and our worth in comparison to others can lead to feelings of inadequacy and insecurity. It prevents us from truly being true to ourselves and to each other's differences. However, we can develop the ability to perceive things for their true nature rather than constantly comparing them to others. We can also break free from this habit and learn to appreciate things for what they truly are.

Additionally, we should always appreciate what we have and be thankful to God for how far He has brought us

(1 Kgs 3:3-6). We tend to forget that it is easy to get caught up in comparing ourselves to others and focusing on what we lack, but it is essential to remember all the blessings God has given us through our Lord and Saviour, Jesus Christ. Gratitude is a powerful practice that can bring overwhelming joy and contentment into our lives. Being thankful and appreciative can nurture a positive mindset and attract even more blessings to our household.

Furthermore, the consequences of unfavourable comparison. If you ever do compare, you should compare where you were with where you are to know what the Lord has done for you. Looking back to the past and present can help you appreciate the progress you've made and the blessings you've received (2 Sam 7:1-17). It's important to acknowledge and celebrate your life's achievements and changes, recognise the Lord's hand in shaping your journey, compare where you were with where you are now, and see the faithfulness and goodness of God in your life.

The best way to improve yourself is to imitate the Lord Jesus Christ. (Philippians 3:7-14). We can demonstrate affection and compassion toward all those around us. In the same way that He was, we can endeavour to be forgiving and kind and to serve others selflessly. He told His disciples that we are the light and hope of the world that needs His grace and mercy to follow His examples. Let us follow in His footsteps, disseminating His message of love and salvation to all who cross our path.

Lastly, it can be tempting to admire and try to emulate the gifts and talents of others. There can be value in doing this. But above all that, we should enhance our own strengths; expanding our knowledge, experiences, and skills. This is the key to our success. Remember that your true self is always more genuine than any persona you attempt to copy. Be diligent in developing yourself to become a better person.

Give yourself wholly to developing yourself, and in no time, *"your profiting may appear to all"* (1 Timothy 4:15).

REFLECTIONS

- Who exactly are you?

- What do you like most about yourself?

3
Know Yourself

Do you really know who you are? How do you prove that?

> "Is there not a cause?"
> **1 Samuel 17:29**

Solon of Athens (630-560 BCE) once said, *"Know thyself and you will find wisdom."* This ancient advice captures the essence of self-knowledge, highlighting the value of understanding oneself as the foundation for personal growth and success. Knowing yourself is about recognizing your values, strengths, and purpose. It serves as the guiding compass for navigating life's challenges and making meaningful decisions.

The Importance of Self-Knowledge

Clearly, the only way to live a meaningful life is to discover yourself and pursue your full potential. Have you, as an individual, determined who you are, your purpose on earth, and your vocation? Many individuals merely *'exist';* they never genuinely embody the person they were meant to be. It is each person's responsibility to discover and embrace their identity fully. By exploring our values, beliefs, and passions, we can better understand who we are and what truly matters to us. Once we have a clear sense of our identity, we can confidently build our lives, making choices that align with our authentic selves.

Knowing Yourself Through Self-Reflection

David from the Bible is a prime example of someone who knew himself. When faced with Goliath's challenge, David did not back down because he had a strong awareness of who he was. He declared his past victories over a lion and a bear, which gave him the confidence to confront the giant. This self-knowledge allowed David to remain resilient and courageous, even when others doubted his abilities. His ability to stay true to his identity and purpose was crucial in fulfilling his destiny.

Aligning with Your Divine Purpose

In the case of Jeremiah, God informed him that He had known him even before he was formed in the womb and that He had designated him as a prophet to the nations (Jeremiah 1:5). This emphasizes that understanding oneself goes beyond physical traits—it includes acknowledging the spiritual purpose and calling that God has placed on each person's life.

Knowing yourself means aligning with your divine purpose and recognizing the unique path that has been laid out for you. It is about comprehending your role in the world and living in a way that is congruent with that understanding. This sense of identity enables you to make choices that reflect your purpose and values, ultimately leading to a life of fulfillment.

The Role of Faith in Self-Knowledge

When the storms of life come, they test your faith and your understanding of who you are. Knowing yourself includes recognizing your vulnerabilities and strengths. Through trials, you can gain a deeper understanding of yourself, strengthening your identity and refining your character. Self-knowledge is not static—it evolves through experiences, both good and bad. This process of self-discovery enables you to build a stronger relationship with God and with yourself.

Becoming the Best Version of Yourself

As stated in Ephesians 2:10, *"We are God's handiwork, created in Jesus Christ for good works."* This indicates that each of us has a specific identity and purpose. By pursuing self-knowledge, we discover the best version of ourselves, allowing us to positively impact the world and overcome life's obstacles. Connecting with the divine purpose set for us enables us to embody our true identity, serve others with love and compassion, and walk in alignment with God's plan.

The Path to Self-Knowledge

Self-knowledge begins with introspection and self-awareness. It involves understanding your strengths, weaknesses, values, and aspirations. This knowledge enables you to set meaningful goals and pursue a life that is in harmony with your true self. It is an ongoing journey that requires dedication and a willingness to confront the deeper questions of existence.

Self-knowledge is a powerful tool for personal transformation and spiritual fulfillment. By knowing ourselves, we gain clarity on our purpose, build resilience in the face of challenges, and experience the joy of living authentically. This is the path to wisdom and the foundation for a life of impact and significance.

REFLECTIONS

Take some time to list out your key strengths, values, and passions. Reflect on how they shape your decisions and guide your actions. Consider whether your current life choices align with these personal attributes.

4
Daily Diligence

Great visions are awesome, but accomplishing daily tasks will guarantee you an awesome future.

> "A man diligent in his business? He shall stand before kings."
>
> ***Proverbs 22:29***

The lenses of the wise, which see far beyond the immediate, unravel the mystery of great destiny, revealing the path ahead with clarity and purpose. They perceive every obstacle as a stepping-stone and every challenge as an opportunity for growth and advancement. With insight and understanding, the wise embrace the complexities of life, meeting them with perseverance and unwavering commitment to their goals. They stay true to their dreams and never lose sight of their ultimate purpose.

Jesus warned, *"Wide is the gate and broad is the way that leads to destruction, and many are those who walk in it."* His counsel is clear: strive to enter *"the narrow gate and difficult way that leads to eternal life"* because *"few are those who find it"* (Matthew 7:13-14). This teaching underscores that success is not merely about having ambitious dreams. Rather, it is about making deliberate efforts—through self-discipline, sacrifice, and preparation—to transform those dreams into reality.

The Key to Turning Goals into Reality

Achieving success is not determined by setting radical goals alone. Joseph's story in Genesis 41:41-45 exemplifies how self-discipline, perseverance, and readiness are crucial for making great aspirations achievable. Self-discipline keeps us focused and motivated, pushing us to sacrifice short-term pleasures for long-term rewards. Meanwhile, preparation ensures that we are ready to seize opportunities when they appear. These essential qualities convert ambitious goals into tangible results.

However, as is often seen in life, people may take misguided actions that lead to unproductive outcomes. Why? Some are unwilling to pay the price for exceptional performance, while others believe that success is predetermined or inevitable. The truth is that every long journey begins with a single step. As Julia A. F. Carney (1823-1908) wisely observed, *"Little drops of water make a mighty ocean."* While grand goals can be inspiring, their sheer magnitude can intimidate and discourage us from taking action.

Incremental Progress Towards Grand Goals

The reality is clear: success demands a well-defined plan with clear objectives and actionable steps. As former US Treasury Secretary Timothy Geithner remarked, *"Plan beats no plan."* Instead of being overwhelmed by the enormity of a vision, focus on daily incremental actions. Each small step you take will accumulate, leading to exponential progress over time. Commit to making small changes each day, and by the end of a year, you will have improved 360 times more than if you had done nothing.

By consistently pursuing small, yet meaningful actions, even the most challenging aspirations can be realized. Success is not achieved overnight but through persistence, discipline, and a clear vision.

REFLECTIONS

- **Embrace Small Steps:** Break down your big goals into smaller, manageable tasks and commit to consistent daily actions. Small efforts accumulate over time, transforming grand dreams into tangible achievements.

5
At Your Doorstep

Dying to get great opportunities at a distance while being unable to see the opportunities at your doorstep is not the best.

> "Better is the sight of the eyes than the wandering of desire."
>
> ***Ecclesiastes 6:9***

Opportunities are abundant in our surroundings, waiting to be discovered by those who are vigilant and open-minded. While people often chase grand opportunities, these are rare and may be outside one's sphere of influence. The key is to cultivate a receptive mindset that enables you to recognize and capitalize on opportunities present in your immediate environment. By doing so, you will gradually identify advantageous situations, people, and environments.

King Solomon captures this concept in Ecclesiastes 9:11:

"The race is not to the swift or the battle to the strong,

nor does food come to the wise or wealth to the brilliantor favor to the learned; but time and chance happen to them all."

The phrase **"happen to them all"** serves as a powerful reminder that opportunities come to everyone, regardless of who you are or where you are located.

The Role of Location and Personal Effort

While your geographical location can shape your experiences and influence the opportunities available to you, it does not solely determine your destiny. Ultimately, it is your responsibility to make decisions that shape your future rather than blaming your environment. With determination and hard work, anyone can transcend the limitations of their surroundings and achieve their aspirations.

As Jim Rohn wisely stated, ***"Your potential is defined by what you make of yourself."*** Success is not about chasing greatness but about adhering to principles that naturally attract it. The Scriptures reinforce this idea in Deuteronomy 28: If we diligently listen to and obey God's commandments, blessings will come to us and overtake us. Therefore, the focus should not be on pursuing greatness but on cultivating a mindset and principles that draw greatness to us.

REFLECTIONS

- **Cultivate a Receptive Mindset:** Stay vigilant and open-minded to recognize opportunities in your immediate surroundings, rather than waiting for grand ones. With a proactive attitude, you'll uncover value where others might overlook it.

6
No Laziness

Chances are not for lazy giants but equipped dwarfs.

> "Because of laziness the building decays ..."
> **Ecclesiastes 10:18**

The saying, *"Idleness is next to ungodliness,"* captures the destructive impact of laziness on a person's aspirations and potential. Laziness not only erodes one's goals but also leaves visible consequences when it destroys what could have been a lifetime of productive labor. A lazy person is often unprepared to navigate life's storms and complexities.

The Apostle Paul addresses this issue in his letter to the Thessalonians, warning against aiding those who refuse to work. He states, *"... if any would not work, neither should they eat."* (2 Thessalonians 3:10). This statement is a reminder that everyone has a responsibility to contribute to their own well-being and that of the community.

Biblical Illustrations of Laziness and Its Consequences

This principle is further illustrated in the *Parable of the Talents* (Matthew 25:24-30). The servant who failed to invest his master's gift was harshly judged and expelled. Jesus referred to this individual as an *"unprofitable servant"* (v. 30). Applying this to our own lives, we learn that success is not granted to those who merely wait for it but to those who actively seek and work for it. It's not about the size of the individual but the size of their determination and drive. Laziness can also hinder our relationship with Jesus Christ and undermine our future blessings.

Laziness and the Illusion of Luck

Laziness often fosters delusion, causing a person to believe that all is well and that life will eventually sort itself out. They hope for 'luck' to intervene, even while doing nothing to achieve their goals. However, as it is wisely said, *"Luck is what happens when preparation meets opportunity."* Serendipity occurs when we are prepared to capitalize on the opportunities that come our way.

The Importance of Preparation: David and Goliath

Instead of lamenting missed opportunities, reflect on how well you have equipped yourself. Are you prepared to seize the chance when it arises? Consider the story of David and Goliath in 1 Samuel 17. Though David had no experience as a warrior, he put forth his background as a shepherd who had defeated lions and bears. His preparation and confidence in his past experiences convinced King Saul to allow him to confront Goliath. The Lord's deliverance of Israel came through David's readiness to act.

The lesson is clear: How are you preparing for the great opportunity you hope for? Success is not a product of luck but of diligent preparation and the readiness to act when the moment arrives.

REFLECTIONS

Take ownership of your circumstances and actively seek opportunities rather than waiting for success to come to you. Understand that your contributions shape not only your future but also the well-being of those around you.

7
Be Focused

Focus is one of the greatest keys to great achievements.

> *"Therefore, when thy eye is single, thy whole body also is full of light."*
> **Luke 11:34**

Are you trying to pursue too many paths to achieve your goals? Child of God, remember that there is only one true path to God. Jesus said, *"No one comes to the Father except through Me"* (John 14:6). Why are you tempted to stray from this truth? Can anyone's counsel truly prevail against God's will? It is essential to recognize that distractions and competing interests can lead you away from your divine purpose and clarity in your journey. In a world filled with numerous opportunities and voices, it's easy to lose focus and spread yourself too thin, diluting your energy and commitment.

The Assurance of God's Sovereignty

Consider the words of Isaiah: *"Have you not

known? Have you not heard? Has it not been told to you from the beginning? Have you not understood from the foundations of the earth? He sits above the circle of the earth... He gives power to the weak... those who wait on the Lord shall renew their strength..." (Isaiah 40:21). Additionally, Psalm 125:1 reminds us, *"Those who trust in the Lord are like Mount Zion, which cannot be shaken but endures forever."* This assurance provides us with the confidence to remain steadfast, even amidst life's uncertainties. Knowing that our foundation is secure in God's sovereignty empowers us to confront challenges without fear, as we trust in His perfect timing and plans for our lives.

The Key to Life Fulfillment

A focused individual is determined and possesses a clear vision of their endeavors. They carefully observe and analyze God's word, ensuring that their actions align with it. A person who maintains focus successfully pursues their course of action, even in the face of unforeseen obstacles. The greatest key to remarkable accomplishments is to stay on the straight path that leads to eternity (Joshua 1:8). This unwavering commitment allows individuals to navigate life's complexities with grace and purpose, knowing they are aligned with their divine calling.

When you possess foresight and triumph over adversity, reaching your intended destination becomes an indisputable certainty. As Paul states in Philippians 3:14, he forgets his past and strives toward the reward God has set for him. Similarly, when we remain focused, we can persevere and achieve our rewards and accomplishments. The path may be fraught with trials, but each step taken in faith brings us closer to our goals. Remember that the journey may not always be easy, but staying true to your purpose will ultimately yield fruitfulness in your life. Embrace the challenges as part of the growth process, and trust that God will equip you with the strength and wisdom needed to fulfill your destiny.

REFLECTIONS

Reflect on your current commitments. Which activities or obligations can you prioritize or let go of to maintain focus on your spiritual and

8

Avoid Distractions

Distraction is the number one reason for failure.

> "But foolish and unlearned questions avoid, knowing that they do engender strifes."
>
> **2 Timothy 2:23**

Why is the devil so eager to distract us with trivial things? As Paul asked the Galatians, "O foolish Galatians, who has bewitched you, that you should not obey the truth?" (Galatians 3:1). Remember, *"Obedience is the highest practical courage."* Therefore, we must cast down *"imaginations and every high thing that exalts itself against the knowledge of God, bringing every thought into captivity to the obedience of Christ"* (2 Corinthians 10:5). We should also avoid *"foolish and unlearned questions, knowing they generate strife"* (2 Timothy 2:23).

Child of God, do not be distracted by worries about what you will eat, what clothes to wear, or where to sleep. Your heavenly Father knows you need all these things (Matthew 6:25-34). Such concerns can divert your attention from your Saviour and Lord, Jesus Christ, who gives strength to the weak and bread to the hungry.

Distractions can pull your focus away from *"looking unto Jesus, the author and finisher of our faith"* (Hebrews 12:2). Do you have an ear to hear what the Spirit says to the churches? (Revelation 2:7, etc.). Distractions have led many astray because they did not diligently listen to the voice of the Lord their God to observe and do according to His word. Distraction is indeed the enemy of focus; it is easy to be swayed from your purpose. Redeem the time, child of God, and persevere in your endeavours to achieve success.

In contemporary culture, numerous factors can distract you from your goals. Among the most significant is the excessive use of social media and other platforms. Make a conscious effort to prioritize your Christian life and how you spend your time. Whether it's the constant barrage of social media notifications, the pressure to conform to societal norms, or the fear of failure, it is easy to lose sight of your goals.

However, by staying focused, setting clear priorities, and surrounding yourself with positive influences, you can overcome these distractions and ultimately achieve your desired success. Remember Romans 12:2: *"Do not be conformed to this world, but be transformed by the renewal of your mind, that by testing you may discern what is the will of God, what is good and acceptable and perfect."* Success is a journey, and transforming and renewing your mind is essential. With perseverance and dedication, you can navigate distractions and reach your full potential. Avoid allowing external factors to

9

Confidence

The best person to know you is you.

> "There came a rich man of Arimathea, named Joseph, who also himself was Jesus' disciple."
>
> **Matthew 27:57**

Are You a Secret Christian?

This is a question only you can answer. Remember that faith is a personal journey, and how you practice your beliefs is entirely up to you. Whether you choose to share your faith openly or keep it private, your relationship with God remains between you and Him.

Navigating Your Faith

Consider the example of Joseph of Arimathea. What holds you back from revealing your faith? If you continue to conceal your good works, they may remain unnoticed. Ultimately, the best person to understand your actions and intentions is you. While others may discuss your Christian conduct, no one knows you better than yourself. It is easy for others to misinterpret your good deeds, but as Jesus said, *"Let your light shine before others, so that they may see your good works and give glory to your Father who is in heaven"* (Matthew 5:16).

Understanding Your Worth

The Apostle Paul wisely advised Timothy, *"Let no man despise thy youth"* (1 Timothy 4:12). You have an intimate knowledge of your true self, so *"take heed to yourself and to the doctrine. Continue in them, for in doing this, you will save both yourself and those who hear you"* (1 Timothy 4:16). As Proverbs 14:10 states, *"Each heart knows its own sorrow," and as Paul noted, "What man knows the things of a man except the spirit of the man which is in him?"* (1 Corinthians 2:11). While others may question your integrity, only you know your deepest aspirations and the truths you hold within,

10
Live in Dignity

Believe it or not, you know yourself better than anybody else.

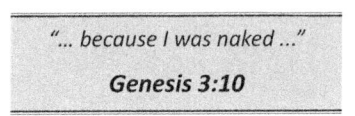

> *"... because I was naked ..."*
> **Genesis 3:10**

Are you still living in sin? As the apostle Paul asked the Galatians, *"O foolish Galatians, who hath bewitched you, that ye should not obey the truth, before whose eyes Jesus Christ hath been evidently set forth, crucified among you?"* (Galatians 3:1). Does sin bring you pleasure? Reflect on this: *"Do ye thus requite the LORD, O foolish people and unwise? Is not he thy father that hath bought thee? Hath he not made thee and established thee?"* (Deuteronomy 32:6).

Remember, it was the disobedience of Adam and Eve that led human endeavours to become *"vanity of vanities"* and *"vexation of spirit"* (Ecclesiastes 1:2; 2:17). Sin will leave you spiritually naked and vulnerable before your enemies, ultimately separating you from your

Maker. The prophet Isaiah warns, *"Behold, the LORD'S hand is not shortened, that it cannot save; nor his ear heavy, that it cannot hear. But your iniquities have separated you from your God"* (Isaiah 59:1-2).

Do you long for freedom from the bonds of sin? Confess your sins and come to Jesus, who promises rest and relief from the burdens that weigh you down (Matthew 11:28). His compassionate love and forgiveness are available to all who seek Him sincerely. Trust in His grace and let go of the guilt and shame that hold you captive. By walking in His word and following His teachings, you will find true peace and redemption. Jesus is the way, the truth, and the life (John 14:6).

As the apostle James asks, *"Who is wise and understanding among you? Let him show by good conduct that his works are done in the meekness of wisdom"* (James 3:13). How do you demonstrate this meekness of wisdom through your actions? Paul advises, *"... by patient continuance in well-doing, seek for glory and honour and immortality ..."* (Romans 2:7).

If you have asked the Lord Jesus to *"anoint your eyes with the eye salve"* so that you can see clearly, remember that no one knows or understands you better than you do. While others may disagree with your decisions, you are the only one who can determine if an action aligns with your true self. Therefore, take courageous steps that fulfil the Lord's purpose for your life on earth.

REFLECTIONS

Consider the consequences of sin in your life. Is it providing temporary pleasure at the expense of your spiritual well-being? Reflect on how it may be creating distance between you and your relationship with God.

11
Spiritual Fortitude

Who can understand you than you?

> *"What you know, I also know; I am not inferior to you."*
>
> **Job 13:2**

Standing firm in your faith and boosting yourself spiritually is crucial when upholding your beliefs and values. As believers, we are called to avoid pointless arguments and controversies that lead to division and strife, recognizing that such disputes are unproductive and do not contribute to spiritual growth. Instead, we are urged to stay rooted in our faith and remain steadfast, unswayed by worldly pressures or temporary circumstances.

We must remember our identity as a chosen generation and a royal priesthood, esteemed and honored by God Himself, regardless of the challenges or opposition we encounter. Our strength lies in the assurance that God is with us through every trial and tribulation, promising that we will not be overwhelmed by the waters or consumed by the fires of life (Isaiah 43:2). This assurance should encourage us to remain strong and courageous, knowing that the Lord never abandons us (Deuteronomy 31:6).

The story of Job serves as a powerful reminder of the importance of unwavering faith and perseverance. Even in the midst of his deepest suffering and perceived silence from heaven, Job held on to his faith, declaring, *"I know that my Redeemer lives"* (Job 19:25). His steadfastness led to a divine restoration and blessings beyond what he had lost, demonstrating that trust in God, even in the darkest moments, is never in vain.

It's crucial to reject any notion of inferiority, as the power of God within us is greater than any worldly force (1 John 4:4). While others may not fully understand us, we possess a unique self-awareness and are called to make decisions grounded in godly wisdom and integrity. Each person's journey is distinct, and what works for others may not necessarily be suited for us. By understanding our own strengths, remaining confident in our God-given abilities, and seeking

God's guidance, we can navigate through challenges and achieve accomplishments that align with His purpose for our lives.

Moreover, we must cultivate a mindset of resilience and a spirit of discernment, recognizing when to stand firm and when to move forward with grace. The Apostle Paul reminds us to *"put on the whole armour of God, that you may be able to stand against the wiles of the devil"* (Ephesians 6:11). This armour includes truth, righteousness, faith, and the Word of God, all of which empower us to confront life's battles with confidence and clarity. As we daily equip ourselves with these spiritual tools, we will not only resist distractions but also remain focused on fulfilling our God-given calling. Embracing this posture allows us to rise above adversities, illuminate our surroundings with Christ's light, and leave a legacy of faithfulness for others to follow.

REFLECTIONS

- **Are you equipping yourself spiritually for the challenges you face, or are you allowing circumstances to dictate your responses?** Remember to wear the full armour of God, aligning your heart and mind with His truth.

- **How can you maintain a strong sense of identity and purpose when opposition arises?** Reflect on God's promises and reaffirm your worth as part of His royal priesthood, standing tall in His strength.

- **What steps are you taking to deepen your faith and spiritual resilience?** Consider how regularly engaging with Scripture, prayer, and spiritual practices can reinforce your courage and enable you to overcome trials like Job did.

12
Self-Doubt

If you doubt yourself, you will destroy yourself.

> "As he thinketh in his heart, so is he."
> Proverbs 23:7

Is thinking beneficial or detrimental? It all depends on what you are focusing your thoughts on! Positive thinking cultivates high self-esteem, self-confidence, boldness, and a 'can-do spirit.' Conversely, negative thinking can produce doubt, low self-esteem, weakness, discouragement, and a pessimistic outlook.

Great thinkers accomplish great things because they never lose sight of the potential within them that the world needs to see. These individuals have the ability to envision new possibilities and bring them to life through risk-taking, innovative ideas, and problem-solving skills. They continuously push the boundaries of what's possible, inspiring themselves and others to think creatively and strive for greatness. In the end, it is the great thinkers who leave a lasting impact on the world and shape the course of history.

The Apostle Paul advises us to focus on what is true, honest, just, pure, lovely, and of good report, saying, *"...if there be any virtue, and if there be any praise, think on these things"* (Philippians 4:8). This instruction underscores the significance of guarding our thoughts because the quality of our life is directly related to the quality of our thoughts. If you fill your mind with negativity and self-doubt, you will inevitably experience a lower quality of life. However, cultivating positive, empowering thoughts and beliefs can result in a more fulfilling and contented life.

When we entertain doubt, we create anxiety and uncertainty about our lives and circumstances. Doubt is often tied to fear. But fear is not from God. When we doubt ourselves, we limit our potential and hinder the magnificent possibilities that lie within us and ahead of us. Thus, it is crucial to trust ourselves and forge ahead with confidence, keeping in mind that great thinking leads to great living. Stay focused on what is good, and you will be more likely to achieve your highest potential.

To elevate the quality of your thoughts, you must take active control over what you feed your mind. What you expose yourself to daily—whether it is through conversations, media, reading material, or social interactions—has a direct impact on your mindset. If you consistently engage with negativity, it will inevitably infiltrate your thought patterns, influencing your perception of yourself and the world around you. Conversely, surrounding yourself with positivity, uplifting messages, and inspiring individuals will nurture a healthy mindset. Make it a habit to meditate on God's promises, focus on your goals, and engage in activities that challenge your intellect and creativity. This will keep your thoughts aligned with your purpose and propel you toward a fulfilling and impactful life.

Moreover, understand that your thoughts are the seeds that determine the harvest of your actions. If you sow seeds of doubt, fear, and worry in your mind, they will manifest as procrastination, stagnation, and missed opportunities in your actions. However, if you plant seeds of faith, courage, and possibility, they will grow into determination, resilience, and accomplishment. Guarding your thoughts, therefore, is not just a mental exercise but a spiritual one. As Proverbs 23:7 states, *"For as he thinks in his heart, so is he."* Choose to think on the best, the brightest, and the boldest outcomes for your life, trusting that with God's guidance, what begins as a positive thought can turn into a remarkable reality.

REFLECTIONS

- **What are the predominant thoughts that occupy your mind daily?** Reflect on whether your thoughts empower you or hinder you. Are they filled with faith and hope, or do they breed negativity and doubt?

- **How do your thoughts align with your aspirations?** Examine if your thought patterns are supporting the goals and dreams you have set for yourself. Are you envisioning success, or are you fixating on potential failures?

- **Are there any mental habits you need to change?** Identify any recurring negative thoughts that might be holding you back. What can you do to replace them with thoughts that affirm your value, purpose, and potential in Christ?

13
Self-Belief

Your ability to trust yourself is the key to your great success.

> *"... to each one according to his ability ..."*
> **Matthew 25:15**

Isn't it amazing that Jesus has so much confidence in us as children of God? This confidence stems from the fundamental truth that God created us in His image and likeness (Genesis 1:26-27). It is also predicated on the Holy Spirit's residence within us due to our acceptance of Jesus Christ as our Lord and Saviour (John 14:15-21). Therefore, as people who are supposed to reflect His image and nature, He wants us to have confidence in ourselves as we trust Him. This model of leadership paves the way for exposure that engenders great opportunities.

According to *Encyclopaedia Britannica,* Mike Tyson, the famous heavyweight boxing champion, was a member of various street gangs in his early years. While he was in a reform school to get his life back, Bobby Stewart, who was then a social worker and a boxing trainer, discovered his potential and linked him to a formidable boxing trainer, Cus D'Amato, who later became his legal guardian.

So it was that, a few years down the line, a street boy became a renowned world boxing heavyweight superstar. Think about this: Would Mike Tyson have joined the group if he had been aware of his potential? I do not believe so. Throughout those years, he was an exceptional individual; however, he was unaware of it.

Discovering your talent is key to unlocking your potential and achieving success. Beyond the initial discovery, it is crucial to have an unwavering belief in your talent. This belief acts as the driving force behind your actions and decisions, propelling you towards an excellent future. Without faith in your own abilities, you cannot harness the full power of your talent or put it to effective use. Belief in your talent fuels your confidence, motivation, and resilience, enabling you to overcome challenges and seize opportunities. It empowers you to invest time and effort in honing your skills, pushing boundaries, and striving for mastery. Therefore, recognising and nurturing your talent, coupled with a strong belief in its value and potential, is essential for achieving personal and professional fulfilment.

Those who possess self-belief have the courage to make decisions and to undertake endeavours with the confidence that they will be successful. This inner confidence acts as a catalyst, enabling them to take bold steps, embrace challenges, and pursue their goals with determination. Their self-assurance allows them to overcome uncertainties and setbacks with resilience, knowing that their trust in the Lord will see them through.

On the other hand, those who lack self-belief often hesitate to take any action toward their goals. Paralysed by the fear of failure, they remain stagnant, unable to move forward and explore their potential. This hesitation can lead to missed opportunities and unfulfilled dreams, as the lack of self-belief becomes a self-imposed barrier to success. Therefore, it is imperative to cultivate self-belief in order to unlock your maximum potential and accomplish significant tasks.

REFLECTIONS

- Reflect on whether you have taken time to identify and appreciate the talents that God has placed in you. How well do you know what makes you exceptional?

- Think about whether you genuinely believe in your God-given abilities or if you have doubts that hold you back. What steps can you take to strengthen your self-belief?

- Examine whether fear or doubt has prevented you from pursuing opportunities. How can you start tackling these areas to ensure you don't miss out on what God has

14

prepared for you?

Labels

You are one of a kind

> *"Who do people say that the Son of Man is?"*
> ***Matthew 16:13***

No matter who you are or where you come from, your true identity remains intact. Martin Luther King Jr. powerfully expressed this in his iconic *"I Have a Dream"* speech in 1963: *"I have a dream that my four little children will one day live in a nation where they will not be judged by the colour of their skin but by the content of their character."* This statement highlights the profound truth that the content of your character is what defines your true essence. Therefore, do not question your identity or character simply because of how others perceive or treat you. Instead, let the principles of God's Word shape and define your character. As the Lord commanded Joshua, *"This Book of the Law shall not depart from your mouth, but you shall meditate on it day and night, so that you may be careful to do according to all that is written in it. For then you will make your way prosperous, and then you will have good success"* (Joshua 1:8).

People may try to impose names and labels on you that do not accurately reflect your true self. Consider the example of Jesus when He asked His disciples, *"Who do people say that I am?"* (Mark 8:27). The responses varied—John the Baptist, Elijah, or one of the prophets. However, these answers did not deter Him because He was not defined by what others thought of Him. It wasn't until Peter declared, *"You are the Christ"* (Mark 8:29), that the truth of His identity was affirmed. Like Jesus, we must drill down until we find the truth about who we are—truth that aligns with God's purpose for our lives. Let God's Word be the mirror that reveals our true character and identity.

When others place inaccurate labels on us or misjudge us, it can be easy to feel discouraged or confused about who we truly are. But we should remember that our confidence should not be shaken by the opinions of others. Our identity is rooted in the character we cultivate through our relationship with God. It is essential to recognize and affirm our God-given identity, allowing our actions and decisions to be guided by this understanding. Knowing who you are in Christ gives you the strength to stand firm and not be swayed by external judgments.

Additionally, it is important to surround yourself with people who affirm your God-given identity and encourage your growth. The opinions and influences of those closest to us can shape our self-perception, so choose relationships that reflect the truth of who God says you are. Seek out mentors, friends, and communities that see your worth and potential in Christ, reminding you of your value when doubts arise.

Moreover, take time to meditate on God's promises and declarations concerning your life. When you internalize His words, you build a strong foundation that reinforces your sense of identity. This practice can be a powerful tool against the voices that attempt to redefine or diminish your worth. Remember, your identity is not a reflection of your circumstances or the views of others; it is rooted in the unchanging truth of who God has created you to be.

Finally, embrace your unique journey with

15

confidence, knowing that God has equipped you for a purpose. There is no need to conform to societal expectations or lose sight of your true self to fit in. Instead, focus on living authentically according to God's plan for your life. When you are true to who you are in Christ, you unlock your full potential and can live a life that truly glorifies Him.

REFLECTIONS

- Evaluate the voices around you—both people and media. Are they building up or tearing down your self-image? Choose to distance yourself from toxic influences and surround yourself with individuals and content that reflect the truth of who you are in Christ.

- Take time to celebrate the milestones and growth in your journey. Each step you take toward becoming more aligned with your God-given identity is worth acknowledging. It's a reminder that God is continuously working in and through you.

Consider the Needy

Don't be selfish; rather, be selfless and mindful of others.

> "When you reap the harvest of your land, you shall not reap your field right up to its edge, neither shall you gather the gleanings after your harvest."
>
> **Leviticus 19:9**

Always keep the needy in your thoughts and actions. Never leave the underprivileged behind. As stated in James 1:27, *"Religion that is pure and undefiled before God the Father is this: to visit orphans and widows in their affliction and to keep oneself unstained from the world."* This is the hallmark of godly individuals who demonstrate compassion and generosity towards those who are less fortunate. They actively seek opportunities to support those in need, going the extra mile to extend a helping hand and uplift the lives of others.

Job exemplified this principle when he said, *"I delivered the poor that cried, and the fatherless, and him that had none to help him."* His declaration was not a boast but rather a testament to his faithfulness to God and a reflection of true religion. Proverbs 19:17 reminds us, *"He who gives to the poor lends to God, and that which he hath given will He pay him again."* Likewise, the Apostle Paul emphasized that remembering the poor is a vital expression of the Gospel (Galatians 2:10). Acts of generosity toward those in need not only enrich the lives of the recipients but also deepen our connection to God.

God, in His wisdom, has aligned Himself with the poor and marginalized. Our generosity toward them is, in essence, our service to God Himself. This relationship reminds us that selfishness is not a characteristic of a religion approved by God; instead, it is an attribute that taints our faith. Every act of selflessness holds profound significance, impacting both the well-being of others and our spiritual growth. When we give, we embody the heart of God, reflecting His love and mercy in a world that often overlooks the vulnerable.

"It is more blessed to give than to receive" (Acts 20:35), and this divine principle is evident throughout Scripture, reinforcing the call to generosity. As we cultivate a mindset of giving, we become instruments of hope and change in our communities. It is essential to remain vigilant and compassionate, especially during times of harvest and abundance, ensuring

that our blessings overflow into the lives of those who are struggling. In doing so, we not only honour our commitments to God but also foster a spirit of unity and love that transcends societal barriers.

Ultimately, cultivating a habit of generosity transforms us and the world around us. When we make it a priority to care for the needy, we create a ripple effect that encourages others to do the same. This cycle of compassion strengthens communities and fosters a culture where kindness and empathy flourish. Let us embrace our role in uplifting the less fortunate, understanding that in giving, we receive far more than we could ever imagine. By prioritizing the needs of others, we align ourselves with the very essence of Christ's teachings and become vessels of His grace in a world yearning for hope and healing.

REFLECTIONS

Take time to assess how your actions affect those around you. Are you making a positive difference in the lives of others? Recognize that even small acts of kindness can have a significant impact. Challenge yourself to perform at least one act of kindness each week.

16
All Die

Dead people cannot exercise faith.

> *"The rich man also died, and was buried."*
> **Luke 16:22**

Death is an undeniable reality that many of us seldom think about or prepare for. We often get caught up in our daily responsibilities—family, mortgage, rent, healthcare, and work. While these concerns are undoubtedly important, it's also essential to remember that death is an inevitable part of life. Regardless of our age, race, gender, or social status, death treats us all equally. It serves as a reminder of our mortality and emphasizes the importance of cherishing each moment we have on this Earth. When faced with death, our differences fade away, leaving only the shared experience of being human. This sobering truth unites us and highlights the fragility of life, prompting us to reflect on what truly matters and to live each day with intention and gratitude. Ultimately, death is the great equalizer, reminding us that we are all mortal beings on a journey through time.

Because death does not discriminate, it is crucial to build our faith in the Lord Jesus Christ while we are alive. We must strive to stay on the right path and not be led astray by distractions that lead to destruction. When the angel of death knocks at your door, it will be too late to seek faith or accept Jesus Christ as your Lord and Saviour. In the parable of the rich man and Lazarus from the Gospel of Luke (16:19-31), both men faced death, illustrating this point. The rich man lived a life of luxury, adorned in fine clothes and indulging in excess, seemingly oblivious to the reality of death that loomed near. In contrast, Lazarus, a beggar covered in sores and longing for scraps from the rich man's table, remained faithful despite his suffering, never losing hope that his situation would one day change.

One striking aspect of this narrative is that Lazarus maintained his faith in the Lord throughout his hardships. He held on to the belief that his suffering was temporary and that rest awaited him. Ultimately, he found peace in the bosom of Abraham. This teaches us not to deny Jesus Christ in the face of pain or adversity. Don't abandon your faith due to unpleasant circumstances. *"Wake up and live,"* for *"Christ will give you light"* (Ephesians 5:14). As long as there is breath in you, God's purpose for your life is not complete.

Sadly, many people live without hope, effectively dead even while they are alive. They fail to recognize or embrace the grace of God in their lives, leading to unfulfilled destinies and dreams. It can be said that cemeteries are filled with brilliant aspirations that never came to fruition. However, your life is meant to be different. You are destined to live fully and purposefully. *"Live a life worthy of the calling you have received"* (Ephesians 4:1). As long as you have breath, there is hope for a brighter tomorrow. There is assurance that everything will work out for your good, and it will (Romans 8:28). Remember, even a tree cut down will sprout again at the scent of water (Job 14:7-9). If you have life and faith in God, you will fulfil your purpose on earth.

Embracing the reality of death can inspire us to live more intentionally, prioritizing what truly matters. It encourages us to cultivate meaningful relationships, engage in acts of kindness, and contribute positively to the lives of others. By recognizing the fleeting nature of time, we can shift our focus from trivial pursuits to significant endeavors that leave a lasting impact. This perspective invites us to pursue our passions wholeheartedly, seize opportunities for growth, and make the most of each moment. Ultimately, a life lived with the awareness of mortality leads to a deeper appreciation for life itself, urging us to create a legacy that reflects the love, faith, and purpose God has instilled in us.

REFLECTIONS

Set aside time each week to reflect on your goals, values, and what truly matters to you. Create a list of actions you can take to align your daily life with these priorities, whether through acts of service, personal development, or pursuing passions that ignite your spirit. By living intentionally and embracing opportunities for growth, you can maximize the impact of your time on Earth and fulfill the purpose you've been called to achieve.

17
One Life

The grave is an irreversible destination; any notion of a return is erroneous.

> *"And as it is appointed unto men once to die, but after this the judgement ..."*
> Hebrews 9:27

Certain world religions uphold the concept of reincarnation. – that when someone dies, they return in another form. According to them, death offers a person a new opportunity to change one's family or nation for the better. In their view, if you lived in poverty, you might experience wealth in your next life, continuing this cycle many times before it ends. Let's assume for a moment that this is indeed so. It remains, however, that, regardless of the number of opportunities or lifespans, the inevitable appointment with death awaits us all. Job puts it well: *"Seeing his days are determined, the number of his months are with thee, thou hast appointed his bounds that he cannot pass"* (Job 14:5). No matter how many lives we might live, our days are ultimately numbered, and we cannot escape our final destiny this side of eternity: death.

Of course, the Word of God tells us that we have only one life on earth this side of eternity. And our days on earth are determined by our Creator. No one can alter this divine plan. It is not within our power, nor within the hands of any other god, to change the places we will go, or the choices we face. This is a divine appointment, an unchangeable truth that all humanity will experience, regardless of their creed, colour, gender, social status, or anything. *"We flourish like flowers, only to be cut down like grass, and soon we vanish like a fleeting shadow, leaving no trace behind"* (Job 14:2).

Despite this unerring certainty, however, no one knows their divinely appointed time. Indeed, there are three things that remain unknown to all of us:

None of us knows *when* we will die.

None of us knows *where* we will die.

None of us knows *how* we will die.

The purpose of this divine appointment is to affirm to all flesh that we are each accountable to God. 2 Corinthians 5:10 states it clearly: *"For we must all appear before the judgement seat of Christ; that everyone may receive the things done in his body, according to that he hath done, whether it be good or bad."* The inevitability of this divine appointment, moreover, underlines the importance of Christ's redemption work.

"To everything there is a season, and a time to every purpose under the heaven: A time to be born, and a time to die ..." (Ecclesiastes 3:1-2). Death is an inevitable part of life, and the final destination of everyone's journey this side of eternity. When you die and are buried in a grave, there is no turning back. All the possibilities of what you could have done or who you could have become come to an end. The grave is not just a final destination, it is an irreversible destination.

Therefore, make it a point to live fully and truly until your last breath. Do not allow your aspirations and purposes to wither away while you are still alive. Do not let sin and unclean acts dominate your life. The time to repent is now; the time to build yourself up and become all that you can be is now. Focus on that, and show up for yourself while you still have time to live. *"So teach us to number our days, that we may gain a heart of wisdom"* (Psalm 90:12).

REFLECTIONS

Embrace each day with intentionality. Create a daily practice of gratitude to remind yourself of the beauty in each day. At the end of each day, take a moment to reflect on what you accomplished, how you made a difference in someone's life, or what you learned.

18
Prepare Ahead

Make plans for the day you will take your last breath

> *"Gather yourselves together, and hear, ye sons of Jacob; and hearken unto Israel, your father."*
>
> **Genesis 49:2**

Supporting a loved one who is terminally ill or at the end of life is incredibly challenging, but it is also a profound opportunity to show your care and presence. Your presence alone can mean the world to them as they are sailing through their final journey. Being there to hold their hand, listen to their fears, and offer comfort can bring immense solace during such a difficult moment. Your unwavering love and support can make all the difference in helping your loved one feel at peace as they approach the end of their life. Nevertheless, their final words and condolences are irreplaceable.

Again, why is your presence so important? Research shows that a dying person experiences a wide range of emotions, including fear, worry, anger, and sadness. These emotions arise because they face uncertainty and helplessness. Your presence can alleviate some of their distress and emotional turmoil. Being there for them can offer peace and a sense of security.

Your presence also provides them with the opportunity to share their thoughts and wishes. They may want to discuss how they envision their funeral, how they hope their legacy will continue, or share personal reflections. Don't wait until it's too late when the person can no longer communicate or get involved.

In their final hours, your presence conveys two critical messages: (1) They are loved, cared for, and respected in their dying moments. (2) Your face-to-face goodbye comforts their soul and spirit. This is especially true if you guide them through a process of prayer, helping them find peace and, if they wish, leading them to Christ.

When my mum died during a trip to Abidjan, she never returned. We didn't know how she died, and this has always haunted me. I often wonder if she needed my support in some way that could have prolonged her life or if she had something important to tell me. The uncertainty, fear, and hopelessness that followed her sudden death taught me valuable lessons.

I learned to understand the feelings of Jesus' disciples in John 14. Jesus prepared His disciples for His death, assuring them of His resurrection and promising to prepare a place for them in His Father's house. He gave them hope and comfort in the face of His imminent departure.

Also, I realised that in end-of-life situations, the responsibility falls on both us and our loved ones. No one can stop death, but we can ensure that our loved ones do not face it alone. Therefore, being there counts a lot.

One way to truly live life is to think from the endpoint of death and work your way backwards. Consider what you want people to say about you at your funeral, how you want to be remembered, and the level of impact you hope to achieve. By contemplating these questions carefully, you can start putting measures in place to ensure that you leave this world gracefully. Thinking about saying goodbye helps you set up systems and actions to create a meaningful legacy.

So, what are you waiting for? Start planning now for how you want to exit this world, and let that inform the kind of life you live today. Live intentionally, with your end goals in mind, to ensure you leave behind a lasting and positive impact.

If you have the chance to be with a loved one at the end of their life, don't let anything hold you back—whether it's a grudge, offence, or any unresolved issue. Find it within yourself to forgive and wish them well. You may not fully understand the significance of this moment, but your presence and forgiveness can offer immense comfort and peace to both you and your loved one.

REFLECTIONS

Prioritize meaningful conversations. Take the time to initiate deep and meaningful conversations with your loved ones about their feelings, memories, and hopes for the future. Set aside distractions and dedicate moments to listen actively and openly. This not only provides them with a safe space to express themselves but also strengthens your connection and creates lasting memories that you both can cherish.

19
Seek Knowledge

Information is food for thought, but knowledge is the light that comes from the word of God.

> "The wise lay up knowledge, but the mouth of a fool brings ruin near."
>
> **Proverbs 10:14**

A thirst for true knowledge cannot be quenched until one finds Christ, the one *"greater than our father Jacob, who gave us the well and drank from it himself, as did also his sons and his livestock."* While seeking to accumulate knowledge to accomplish your dreams is commendable, no one can lead you to the fountain of knowledge that truly satisfies the wise soul except Christ Jesus. What, then, is knowledge? The *Oxford Dictionary* defines knowledge as *"the information, understanding, and skills that you gain through education or experience."* This definition encompasses the efforts to amass knowledge through various encounters, credentials, titles, achievements and experience. However, these great efforts do not by themselves make one wise.

"Who is wise and understanding among you? Let them show it by their good life, by deeds done in the humility that comes from wisdom" (James 3:13). Where is the path to this humility of wisdom? *"Oh, the depth of the riches and wisdom and knowledge of God! How unsearchable his judgments, and his paths beyond tracing out!"* (Romans 11:33). This path is the fear of the Lord, which the wise lay up in their hearts.

The text illustrates that the knowledge of the wise goes beyond mere achievements. As the proverb states, *"The fool says in his heart, 'There is no God'"* (Psalm 53:1). Information is raw data available to everyone, but not everyone understands that information alone is not enough. Knowledge emerges when information is analysed and its patterns or strategies are derived. This highlights that while information can be thought about, it does not have a material or incremental impact on our lives unless it is understood and applied. Proverbs 18:15 says, *"The heart of the discerning acquires knowledge, for the ears of the wise seek it out."* This indicates that to be considered wise, one must seek and acquire knowledge.

Knowledge is light because it broadens one's understanding and helps identify ways to improve oneself. Therefore, in all your pursuits, seek knowledge and understanding. To be wise, one must begin with acquiring wisdom from the Word of God. Without this foundation, no amount of knowledge can make a person wise. As said by the Apostle Paul, *"the wisdom of God is foolishness to the lost"* (1 Corinthians 1:25), but to the wise, *"we impart a secret and hidden wisdom of God, which God decreed before the ages for our glory"* (1 Corinthians 2:7).

The hidden wisdom of God cannot be found anywhere else but in Christ Jesus. As Augustine of Hippo said, *"For Thou hast made us for Thyself and our heart is restless until it finds its rest in Thee."*

The hidden wisdom of God cannot be found anywhere else but in Christ Jesus. As Augustine of Hippo said, *"For Thou hast made us for Thyself and our heart is restless until it finds its rest in Thee."* In this light, seeking true knowledge is not just an academic pursuit; it is a spiritual journey that transforms the heart and mind. Embracing the truth found in Christ enables us to navigate life's complexities with discernment and grace. This divine knowledge empowers us to make choices that reflect our values and beliefs, fostering a life of purpose and fulfillment that echoes beyond our earthly existence.

REFLECTIONS

Prioritize spiritual growth: Make it a point to dedicate time each day to read and reflect on the Word of God. Consider starting a journal to document insights, prayers, and revelations you receive during this time. This practice will not only deepen your understanding of spiritual wisdom but also help you apply biblical principles to everyday decisions, fostering a life that reflects Christ's teachings.

Seek knowledge through community: Engage with a community or group that prioritizes spiritual and intellectual growth. This could be a Bible study group, a book club focusing on Christian literature, or a mentorship relationship with someone whose wisdom you admire. Sharing perspectives and experiences with others will enrich your understanding and help you apply the knowledge of God in practical ways, building a support system that encourages continuous learning and growth.

20
True Knowledge

True knowledge of Christ is the vehicle of destiny.

> "By Knowledge shall the chambers be filled with all precious and pleasant riches."
>
> ***Proverbs 24:4***

A Lesson in Value

Years ago, a relative gifted me a bracelet with the suggestion that I keep it for my future wife. At the time, neither of us understood its true worth. I held onto it for years until curiosity led me to have it tested. To my surprise, I discovered it was made of gold and held significant value. I initially thought my relative was unaware of its worth; otherwise, he wouldn't have given it to me. However, when I informed him of its true value, he took the gift back, revealing a deeper lesson.

The Cost of Ignorance

This experience taught me a powerful lesson: ignorance can be costly. My relative unknowingly gave away something precious because he didn't recognize its value. This scenario is a reminder that ignorance can have greater consequences than knowledge. Are you aware of the true value of Christ Jesus? Have you embraced the greatest gift from God? When you truly *"taste"* Him, you discover that He is gracious and merciful. He provides rest for the weary soul and strength to the faint. He is the river of life, and those who drink from Him will never thirst again.

The Pursuit of Knowledge

In today's fast-paced world, ignorance is a barrier to success. Some may argue that ignorance is bliss, but that statement is gravely misleading. Ignorance is not bliss; it is a significant hindrance that can prevent you from fulfilling your destiny. With the wealth of information available online, learning opportunities are virtually limitless. However, to benefit from this knowledge, you must first determine your goals and aspirations. Understanding what you want to achieve will help guide your pursuit of knowledge and empower you to reach your potential.

The Key to Success

Knowledge is the key that separates the successful from the unsuccessful. It enables the wise to see further than those who are uninformed. Ignorance blinds individuals to opportunities and possibilities. Therefore, it is essential to seek out and accumulate the true knowledge of the wise, which can take you as far as your dreams can envision. Embrace the pursuit of knowledge with purpose and intention. Let it empower you to become the best version of yourself, fulfilling your purpose and destiny in life.

Embracing Wisdom

It is crucial to recognize that knowledge is not merely an accumulation of facts; it is an understanding that informs your choices and shapes your character. As you navigate through life, remember that wisdom is found in the pursuit of understanding, especially in relation to your faith. The greater your awareness of Christ and His teachings, the more equipped you are to make decisions that reflect your values and aspirations. Seek knowledge, embrace wisdom, and allow it to guide your journey towards fulfillment and purpose.

REFLECTIONS

Set aside some time to reflect on the areas of your life where you may be lacking knowledge or understanding. Identify specific goals or aspirations you wish to achieve and research the necessary information, skills, or insights needed to reach them. Create a plan to acquire this knowledge through reading, online courses, or seeking mentorship.

21
Face Failure

Failure can be managed.

> *"Let us break their bands asunder, and cast away their cords from us."*
> **Psalm 2:3**

Our world has reached a point where strategy, principles, and intelligence are replacing God's supremacy and His divinity. We quickly forget what Jesus said to Nicodemus in John 3:12: *"What is born of the flesh is flesh, and what is born of the Spirit is spirit."* We fail to remember that *"by strength, no man prevails."* Yet, the wisdom of this age continually demonstrates a belief that we can, without fail, fix our chaotic world and make it better without Christ Jesus.

Oh man, how long will it take for you to learn your lesson? Remember when you declared, *"Come, let us build ourselves a city and a tower with its top in the heavens, and let us make a name for ourselves, lest we be dispersed over the face of the whole earth."* Were you able to finish it, oh man? The Lord laughed and scattered you all over the face of the earth. Since then, your strategies, principles, and intelligence have led you to seek to rule, manipulate, intimidate, and dominate over your own kind instead of loving your neighbour as yourself.

Our reliance on earthly wisdom and strength has led us astray. It has caused us to forget the need for the divine guidance and power that comes from Christ Jesus. True transformation and healing in our world come from embracing the spiritual truths that Christ taught. Only by returning to these principles can we hope to create a world that reflects His love and righteousness.Top of FormBottom of Form

Failure occurs when one fails to recognise Christ Jesus as the Lord and Saviour in all endeavours. However, when one fails, it is not the end. Failure can serve as an awakening, empowering you to change your ways and, consequently, your circumstances. For believers, Psalm 145:14 reminds us, "The Lord upholds all who fall." This may signify failures in various areas of our lives, but when we recognise and acknowledge our failures, we gain a clearer perspective on how to work towards success. By praying to God for guidance and direction, we can embark on our journey towards success through our Lord and Saviour, Jesus Christ.

Failure, therefore, is not a final destination but a stepping stone. It is an opportunity to reassess, refocus, and realign with God's purpose for our lives. With faith and perseverance, we can transform our setbacks into comebacks, trusting that God upholds us and leads us toward a brighter and more prosperous future.

A Call to Humility

In our pursuit of success, it is essential to approach our ambitions with humility. We must recognize that our plans and strategies can only take us so far without acknowledging God's sovereignty. As Proverbs 16:9 states, *"The heart of man plans his way, but the Lord establishes his steps."* This verse serves as a reminder that while we may have aspirations and goals, it is God who ultimately directs our paths. When we submit our plans to Him, we open ourselves to divine intervention and guidance that can lead us to outcomes far beyond our limited understanding. Humility invites us to lean not on our understanding but to seek wisdom from above, allowing God's purposes to unfold in our lives.

The Power of Surrender

Surrendering to Christ is not a sign of weakness; rather, it is the ultimate display of strength and trust. By acknowledging our limitations and the futility of relying solely on human wisdom, we create space for God's power to work in us and through us. In 2 Corinthians 12:9, Paul reminds us, *"My grace is sufficient for you, for my power is made perfect in weakness."* Embracing our weaknesses allows us to experience God's grace and strength in profound ways. When we surrender our plans and ambitions to Him, we discover a path filled with purpose and fulfillment, transforming our failures into testimonies of His faithfulness. Ultimately, it is in our vulnerability that we find true strength, realizing that our worth and success are rooted in our relationship with Christ rather than our accomplishments.

22
Born to Win

Everyone is born to win

> *"My frame was not hidden from you, when I was being made in secret, intricately woven in the depths of the earth."*
>
> **Psalm 139:15**

You are born a winner, uniquely equipped by God with special abilities and gifts that set you apart from the rest. Many individuals may not fully realise their potential or acknowledge the hard work, determination, and faith required to achieve success. Proverbs 22:29 underscores the value of diligence: *"Seest thou a man diligent in his business? He shall stand before kings; he shall not stand before mean men."* With unwavering dedication and perseverance, you can overcome any obstacle in your path. Remember, the only limits that truly exist are those we impose on ourselves. Step boldly into the world, pursue your dreams, and embrace the truth that you were born to win.

God created each of us wonderfully and uniquely among billions on earth. You are fearfully made, unparalleled, and unmatched in every way. Your very existence reflects His craftsmanship, from the intricate details of your fingerprint to the uniqueness of your voice and appearance. Don't let doubt or the lies of the enemy convince you otherwise. You are not useless or hopeless; you are destined for greatness. Before you were born, God ordained you a winner. It's essential to discover and embrace your true self; this is the secret to your winning journey. Your uniqueness is not just a blessing; it is a powerful tool for your purpose in life.

Why then should your spirit be downcast? *"Arise, shine, for your light has come, and the glory of the Lord rises upon you"* (Isaiah 60:1). God comforts the downtrodden and fills them with His Spirit, endowing them with ability, intelligence, knowledge, and craftsmanship to fulfil their purpose and overcome challenges. When you recognise that you are a vessel of God's glory, your perspective shifts. Instead of focusing on your limitations, you begin to see the possibilities that lie ahead. Each day becomes an opportunity to shine your light and share your gifts with the world.

Regardless of your background, family connections, or wealth, you are born to win. Each of us possesses unique abilities and talents deposited by God through Jesus Christ. Even if circumstances suggest otherwise, 1 John 5:4 assures us that *"everyone born of God overcomes the world."* As believers, we are already victorious through our faith in Christ Jesus. This victory is not contingent upon external validation or circumstances but is rooted in our identity as children of God. Therefore, cultivate a mindset of victory and let it shape your reality—you are a born winner.

To fully realise your potential, you must first believe in yourself and your capabilities. Self-doubt can be crippling, but understanding your worth in Christ can empower you to overcome these mental barriers. Regularly remind yourself of your gifts and the unique contributions you bring to the world. Surround yourself with supportive individuals who uplift and encourage you. As you build a community of positivity around you, your self-belief will grow, and you will be better equipped to face life's challenges.

Winning is not merely a state of mind; it requires action. Begin to set clear, achievable goals that align with your passions and talents. Create a plan to reach these goals, and take consistent steps towards them. Remember that each small step is a victory in itself. By being proactive in pursuing your dreams, you demonstrate your commitment to living out your purpose. When you take action with faith and determination, you are not just hoping to win; you are actively participating in the success that God has already ordained for you.

REFLECTIONS

Reflect on Your Unique Gifts: Take some time to identify and write down your unique abilities, talents, and experiences that set you apart. Consider how these gifts can be used to serve others and contribute to your community. Reflect on any doubts or limitations you've placed on yourself and challenge those thoughts by affirming your worth as a child of God. Embrace the truth that you are uniquely crafted for greatness and that your journey is meant to shine a light in the world.

23
You Will Not Fail

You are not born a failure.

> "I will not leave you desolate"
> **John 14:18**

The philosophies of failure and success can indeed vary based on individual perspectives, but having the assurance of divine support offers a distinctive perspective. *"I will not leave you desolate,"* assures the Lord to those who place their faith in Him. This promise signifies that we are never alone in our times of need and our search for answers in this life; God stands by our side, providing us with strength and comfort. With Him, we can confidently face any challenges that come our way, knowing His guidance will lead us through.

In today's society, there is often pressure to achieve certain milestones, yet it's crucial to recognise that each person's journey is different. Viewing failure as a learning opportunity can shift our mindset toward eventual success, especially when we hold onto the assurance that *"let not your heart be troubled"* with God's presence.

As we continue to face setbacks and difficulties, we can find comfort in knowing that God's presence and strength will carry us through. Resilience and perseverance are also essential in overcoming barriers and achieving life goals. Consider an individual born into extreme poverty, facing systemic barriers that make success seem insurmountable. Even in such circumstances, as Jacob told Esau, there is a promise of breaking free from oppressive yokes through God's intervention. With God, nothing is impossible; He hears our cries and responds.

Acknowledging systemic barriers and external challenges is crucial, as they can significantly impact one's ability to succeed. However, it's also vital to recognise personal agency and the role of determination in navigating these obstacles. While external factors pose challenges, our determination and ability to adapt to circumstances, coupled with seeking divine guidance, can lead to breakthroughs.

No one is born to fail; God has a purpose for

each of us before we were even conceived. God's intentionality ensures that our existence is not in vain; He has plans for our success and fulfilment. If challenges arise in tasks He has called us to, it's a call to persevere, not a sign of failure. Embrace this truth: you are not a mistake. God doesn't make mistakes, and He did not create you to fail. Therefore, declare with confidence, *"I am born to win, and I am not a failure."* Trust in His plan, for His promises endure forever.

In our pursuit of success, it's vital to understand that our paths are often shaped by both our circumstances and our choices. Embracing the belief that we are destined for greatness empowers us to take control of our narratives. When we confront challenges with the conviction that we are divinely supported, we can transform obstacles into stepping stones. Each setback is not merely a hindrance but a part of our growth, teaching us resilience and deepening our faith. As we navigate through life's complexities, we must remember that our experiences, whether perceived as failures or successes, are integral to fulfilling our purpose.

Moreover, faith is not just about waiting for divine intervention; it's about actively participating in the process of achieving our goals. It calls us to align our actions with our beliefs, stepping forward with courage even in the face of uncertainty. By trusting God and taking actionable steps toward our dreams, we invite His guidance into our lives. This partnership enables us to harness our unique gifts and abilities, propelling us forward on our journey. Let this be a reminder that while success may not always look the way we expect, with faith and determination, we can overcome any hurdle and ultimately fulfill the purpose God has designed for us.

REFLECTIONS

- Consider how you can shift your perspective on setbacks in your life. Rather than viewing them as failures, reflect on how they can serve as valuable lessons that contribute to your personal growth and resilience. Ask yourself: What have I learned from my challenges, and how can I use these lessons to propel myself forward?

- Reflect on the ways you can take proactive steps in your life that align with your faith. Identify specific actions you can take to pursue your goals while trusting in God's guidance. How can you incorporate prayer, scripture, or spiritual practices into your daily routine to strengthen your faith and enhance your determination to succeed?

24
Pursue Mastery

Mastery is key.

> "He teacheth my hands to war;So that mine arms do bend a bow of brass."
>
> **Psalm 18:34**

Achieving mastery in a specific skill or field can be a challenging but rewarding journey. David's approach to mastery, guided by the mentorship of the Lord's teachings, exemplifies a profound dedication to excellence. His ability to metaphorically bend the bows of brass, symbolising his victories over enemies, underscores the effectiveness of divine wisdom in his pursuits. David's success in battle illustrates the power of learning and applying spiritual principles to practical situations.

Many seek mastery through mentorship from experts, learning from their experiences and guidance. Others prefer a self-directed path, utilising resources like online courses, books, and practice to hone their abilities. Regardless of the approach, dedication, persistence, and a continuous thirst for learning are essential elements of achieving mastery. Through consistent practice, experimentation with different methods, and a commitment to growth, individuals can unlock their full potential and excel in their chosen fields.

Consistency and dedication are pivotal in the pursuit of mastery. The Book Proverbs warns against the desire of the slothful, emphasising that success requires diligent effort. The Book Galatians reminds us that perseverance in well-doing leads to a harvest of success, reinforcing the importance of enduring commitment to our goals. The Bible, which is often referred to as *"the manual of life,"* encourages these virtues as foundational to progress and great achievement.

While mastery is crucial for success, it's essential to acknowledge that God-given talent, natural abilities, and divine favour also play significant roles. Psalm 127:1 highlights the importance of God's involvement in our endeavours, underscoring that human efforts alone can be futile without His guidance and blessing.

However, focusing solely on mastery can potentially limit creativity and innovation. The proverb *"by strength shall no man prevail"* cautions against relying solely on personal efforts. The adage *"jack of all trades, master of none"* suggests that spreading oneself too thin across various pursuits may hinder deep expertise in a specific area. Thus, while mastery is paramount, balance is necessary to nurture creativity and explore diverse interests without diluting focus.

Successful individuals often demonstrate hyper-focus and dedication to refining their skills in one primary area. For instance, Lionel Messi's unparalleled success in football stems from his singular dedication and relentless pursuit of excellence in the sport. His achievements serve as a testament to the power of mastery in maximising potential and achieving extraordinary results.

While pursuing mastery requires unwavering dedication and focus, it's crucial to balance this with openness to divine guidance, creativity, and exploration. By aligning our efforts with God's wisdom and principles and focusing on developing our inherent strengths, we can cultivate mastery that leads to enduring success and fulfilment in our endeavours.

REFLECTIONS

- **Balance Mastery with Openness to Divine Guidance**: Reflect on your journey toward mastering a specific skill or field. Are you dedicating enough time to seek God's guidance and wisdom in your pursuits? Consider how you can integrate prayer or meditation into your practice, allowing divine insight to inspire your learning and creativity.

- **Cultivate a Growth Mindset**: Mastery is not just about perfecting skills but also about embracing the learning process. Reflect on how you view setbacks or challenges in your journey. Instead of seeing them as failures, consider them as opportunities for growth and refinement. How can you adopt a mindset that welcomes experimentation and adaptation as essential components of achieving excellence?

25
Yes, You Can

"I can't" is the language of losers.

> "I can do all things through Christ which strengtheneth me."
> ***Philippians 4:13***

The journey from *"I can't"* to *"I can"* is indeed transformative and rooted in faith, determination, and a belief in one's potential through Christ Jesus. Barack Obama's historic presidency, symbolised by the slogan *"Yes, we can,"* exemplifies how faith and perseverance can overcome seemingly insurmountable obstacles. It captions the truth that, *"with God, all things are possible,"* and challenges are merely distractions on the path to achieving one's dreams.

Scripture provides profound encouragement in times of struggle and doubt. Jesus' invitation in Matthew 11:28 to come to Him for rest resonates deeply, offering solace and strength to those burdened by challenges. Zechariah 4:6 reinforces the idea that success is not achieved by human might or power alone but by the guidance and empowerment of the Holy Spirit.

The Apostle Paul's example illustrates how faith in Christ Jesus empowers believers to endure hardships and achieve greatness. Despite facing numerous trials on his missionary journeys, Paul relied on God's grace and love to traverse adversity and fulfil his calling. His unwavering faith serves as a testament to the transformative power of believing in God's plan and persevering through difficulties.

Prayer becomes a powerful tool in aligning with God's purpose and receiving His guidance. Acknowledging God's presence and love in our lives, we affirm our belief that we are unstoppable with Him by our side. Through prayer, we seek strength, wisdom, and courage to step out of our comfort zones, fulfil our callings, and overcome diverse challenges.

Addressing limiting beliefs, such as saying *"I can't,"* involves recognising the impact of language on our thoughts and actions. The words we speak shape our reality, influencing how our minds perceive challenges and opportunities. Replacing self-limiting phrases with affirmations of faith and determination, we align our thoughts with God's promises and open ourselves to His guidance in achieving our goals.

Ultimately, moving from a mindset of defeat to one of victory requires embracing the truth of Scripture, trusting in God's plan, and affirming our ability to overcome through Christ, who strengthens us. Removing *"I can't"* from our vocabulary and replacing it with faith-filled declarations, we position ourselves to embrace God's limitless possibilities for our lives and live out our purpose with courage and conviction.

REFLECTIONS

Are you often inclined to say *"I can't"* or doubt your abilities? Consider how these self-limiting phrases impact your mindset and actions. Challenge yourself to replace negative language with faith-filled declarations, such as *"With God, I can overcome this."* How can you cultivate a habit of speaking positively and affirmatively, trusting in God's power to help you achieve your goals?

26
Resilience

Never say it's over when you fail

> *"For there is hope for a tree, if it be cut down, that it will sprout again, and that its shoots will not cease."*
>
> **Job 14:7**

The Power of Hope

Hope is your lifeline, especially in the darkest of times; it serves as the beacon that guides us through storms and challenges. Hold onto it tightly, for it will carry you through even the toughest moments. Remember, as long as there is hope, there is always a chance for a better tomorrow. So, don't lose hope. Keep fighting, maintain your faith in Christ, and keep hoping. In the midst of trials, let hope be the light that illuminates your path, leading you to new beginnings and opportunities.

Renewal Through Christ

Just like a tree that hopes to sprout again after being cut down (Job 14:7), there is hope for us even in our darkest moments. You can rise from your struggles and start anew in Jesus' mighty name. Holding onto hope in Christ means that there is always the possibility of a fresh start and a brighter future (John 10:10). No matter how difficult your circumstances may seem, remember the Author and Finisher of our faith, the Lord Jesus Christ, who empowers us to adapt and overcome. Our darkest moments often reveal our true strength and resilience. So, hold onto hope in Christ Jesus and elevate your faith, knowing that just as a tree blooms again after being cut down, you too can experience renewal and bounce back in the face of your challenges.

Seeking Guidance and Reassessing

If you need help with problems in your career or dreams, seek guidance from the Lord. Reflect on whether it's worth persevering or if a new direction is required. Remember, persistence and determination are crucial, but it's also wise to reassess and redirect your efforts after multiple failures. As Proverbs 24:16 reminds us, the righteous may fall seven times but rise again; bouncing back is the path to breakthrough success. Learn from challenges, process your emotions, and maintain a positive attitude. Trust in the Lord and in yourself, for self-belief and confidence are key to achieving great outcomes.

Embracing Failure as a Teacher

Even if success isn't immediate, failure doesn't define you. Learn from each attempt, as Thomas Edison did in his pursuit of the light bulb. Imagine if he had given up after his first failure—he wouldn't have achieved his groundbreaking innovation. Each setback can serve as a valuable lesson, helping you refine your approach and build resilience. Stay persistent, pick yourself up after failures, and keep striving toward your goals.

The Journey of Hope and Perseverance

Success may take time, but with hope, faith, and perseverance, you can overcome obstacles and achieve your dreams. The journey may not always be straightforward, but each step forward is a testament to your strength and determination. Embrace the process, celebrate small victories, and remember that every effort brings you closer to your aspirations. Trust that God has a purpose for your journey, and with hope as your anchor, you will navigate through life's challenges and emerge victorious.

REFLECTIONS

Take a moment to identify a specific challenge or setback you are currently facing. Write down how this situation has made you feel and any limiting beliefs that may have arisen as a result. Then, shift your focus to hope and possibility by listing at least three affirmations or actions you can take to move forward. Remind yourself that, like the tree that can bloom again, you too have the strength to rise from this situation. Commit to taking at least one action this week that aligns with your affirmations and demonstrates your belief in a brighter future.

27
No Place For Ignorance

Ignorance is the cause of many painful mistakes.

> "And the times of this ignorance God winked at;but now commanded all men everywhere to repent."
> **Acts 17:30**

The consequences of ignorance can be profound and far-reaching in our lives. Many painful mistakes and issues stem from a lack of knowledge or understanding about various matters. Life can be devastated, and situations can be flipped into unbearable conditions due to ignorance. Often, misunderstandings and conflicts arise because people act without fully understanding the consequences of their actions. This lack of awareness can lead to destroying families, hurt feelings, damaged relationships, and unnecessary emotional stress. If we take the time to consider how our actions impact others, we can prevent misunderstandings and conflicts from occurring in the first place. Effective communication, empathy, and self-awareness are vital components in ensuring positive and productive interactions with others.

As a Christian, the essence of being born again is pivotal to your faith journey. It signifies a spiritual transformation and a new beginning in your relationship with God and others. Being born again gives you a more deeper sense of purpose and joy in fellowship with Christ and others. It is a reminder of God's grace and love for you and through you to others, as well as the constant renewal and growing up that comes from surrendering your life to Him.

Apostle Paul emphasises the importance of knowing Christ and urges repentance for those ignorant of His teachings. It is crucial to educate ourselves about Christ Jesus and strive to understand different perspectives to avoid unnecessary complications and spiritual blindness. If we seek knowledge and understanding through God's word, we can deepen our relationship with Him and everyone around us and grow closer to Him (2 Cor 5:17-21). Through learning Christ's teachings and the experiences of others, we can gain valuable insights that can help us sail through challenges and make decisions in alignment with God's will. Educating ourselves about the love of Christ Jesus always enables us to live a more fulfilling and purposeful life.

Wisdom, as expressed in the Book of Proverbs, highlights the value of seeking understanding: *"For whoever finds me finds life and obtains favour from the LORD, but he who fails to find me injures himself; all who hate me love death"* (Proverbs 8:35-36). Ignorance, therefore, is not an excuse. We are accountable for our actions in life, and eventually, we will all stand before the judgment seat of Christ to give an account of how we lived (2 Corinthians 5:10).

Proverbs 22:3 further emphasises the importance of prudence and seeking wisdom: *"The prudent sees danger and hides himself, but the simple go on and suffer for it."* Those who neglect to seek knowledge and counsel are often the ones who find themselves facing unnecessary difficulties and challenges.

Therefore, let us be encouraged to seek wisdom, to educate ourselves, and to avoid the pitfalls of ignorance. If we are open-minded and willing to learn, we can journey through life's complexities with greater clarity and understanding.

REFLECTIONS

Consider a recent situation where a lack of knowledge or misunderstanding led to conflict or distress in your life. Reflect on the actions or decisions that contributed to this outcome and how being more informed or empathetic could have changed the situation. Take a moment to write down the lessons you learned from this experience and how you can apply this newfound understanding to future interactions. Commit to seeking knowledge actively—whether through studying scripture, engaging in meaningful conversations, or educating yourself on different perspectives.

28

Keep Moving

Don't call it done until you get it done.

> "In all toil, there is profit."
>
> **Proverbs 14:23**

Although *victory rarely comes overnight, it is important to remain focused.* The journey may be *long, complex and difficult,* but the outcome of patience and determination is *always worth it.* Remember that *"in all toil, there is profit."* Isaiah 51:7 says, *"you who know righteousness, the people in whose heart is my law; fear not the reproach of man, nor be dismayed at their revilings."* The Lord is with you always and forever, guiding your steps and protecting you from every harm. Stand firm in your faith in Christ Jesus, and do not waver in the face of opposition, for your faith will sustain you through any trials and temptations that may come your way. Trust in the Lord and let His word be your anchor in times of trouble, as the three Hebrew boys stood by their trust in their God and overturned the laws of Babylon.

King Nebuchadnezzar threw them into a fiery furnace. However, to everyone's amazement, they emerged from the furnace unharmed; the fire could not overpower them because they were protected by a fourth figure that appeared to be an angel of the Lord. This miraculous event solidified their trust and devotion to their God, making the people of Babylon have unwavering trust in God and believe in His power. Even King Nebuchadnezzar himself was moved by their courage and faith, and he acknowledged the greatness of their God. This event encourages us not to be shaken by the criticisms or negativity of others. Therefore, keep pushing forward with determination despite any discouragement or adversities.

Proverbs 14:23 reinforces this by stating, *"In all toil there is profit, but mere talk tends only to poverty."* Hard work and persistence lead to victory, guided by God's blessings. Stay patient and steadfast in pursuing your goals. Know that you are stronger than you realise; God is closer than you can ever imagine, and others' opinions cannot define your worth. Stand firm in your convictions, keeping the word of the Lord in your heart.

Remember, the path to victory often requires sacrifice and dedication. Just like a student doctor who sacrifices social activities to focus on studying and stay committed to their goals despite challenges and distractions. They persevere through difficulties in learning and staying focused. That is how they achieve their desired outcomes and celebrate their hard-earned success.

However, humiliations and failures are inevitable on the road to greatness. When faced with failure, it's vital to take responsibility for your actions without letting setbacks define you personally. Learn from mistakes, reflect, and restart with renewed determination. Resilience in the face of failure distinguishes those who achieve greatness.

Take inspiration from Peter in the Bible, who, despite denying Christ three times, sought forgiveness and became a foundational figure in Christianity. His story teaches us that setbacks do not determine our future; rather, our resilience and faith do.

Therefore, do not be discouraged by failures or humiliations. Embrace them as opportunities for growth, excellence and renewal. Keep moving forward with faith, determination, and a commitment to victory. Success awaits those who persevere with unwavering resolve.

REFLECTIONS

Think about a recent failure or setback you experienced. Instead of viewing it as a personal defeat, assess the situation objectively. What could you have done differently, and what insights did you gain from the experience? Recognize that setbacks are not the end but opportunities for growth and renewal. Write down one actionable step you can take to bounce back with renewed determination and faith, just as Peter did after his denial of Christ.

29

Above Your Peers

Investment in learning is the best economic strategy

> "Meditate upon these things; give thyself wholly to them; that thy profiting may appear to all."
>
> **1 Timothy 4:15**

When one invests in attaining knowledge, they are setting themselves above their peers. Knowledge is a powerful tool that can open great and effectual doors to new opportunities and broaden one's perspective. If you constantly seeking to learn the word of God and grow in it, you can stay ahead in your field and adapt to ever-changing circumstances.

Investing in knowledge is a profound investment in oneself, leading to personal and professional development. Anyone can unlock new opportunities and see their complete potential by continuing to invest in knowledge and skills. This ongoing pursuit of knowledge increases one's value in the workplace and enriches one's personal life, promoting a sense of empowerment and joy. In an increasingly competitive environment, it is essential to invest in knowledge in order to remain relevant and adaptable.

Jesus' words in John 8:32 highlight the impact of knowledge on our liberation. The acquisition of knowledge empowers critical thinking, enhances problem-solving skills, and improves communication abilities, all of which are essential in handling contemporary challenges and seizing opportunities for advancement.

In our fast-paced world, those committed to continuous learning are better equipped to adapt and thrive amidst challenges and difficulties. This investment isn't just economically prudent; it also enriches us spiritually. As Apostle Paul advises in Colossians 3:1-2, focusing on heavenly wisdom complements our earthly pursuits, enhancing our ability to improve and excel. In continually seeking wisdom, we enhance our earning potential, job prospects, and personal fulfilment.

Moreover, learning opens doors to new experiences, broadens perspectives, and fosters self-discovery. It contributes to our overall well-being, making us more adaptable and resilient. The wisdom extolled in the Book of Proverbs, particularly in Proverbs 8:1-36, highlights how understanding and knowledge lead to prosperity and spiritual enlightenment. This pursuit of wisdom fuels curiosity, sparks creativity, and enriches our lives with meaning.

Proverbs 4:7 emphasises that wisdom is invaluable, suggesting that the pursuit of knowledge is worth every sacrifice. Daniel and his friends in Daniel 1:17-20 exemplify this principle through their exceptional wisdom, which elevated them to positions of influence and importance in Babylonian society. Their story illustrates how investing in learning can lead to personal success and enable individuals to positively impact the world around them.

Therefore, by investing in knowledge and wisdom, we not only equip ourselves for personal growth and prosperity but also fulfil our potential to influence and shape the world for the better. This commitment to continuous learning is a testament to our dedication to excellence and our journey towards a more enriched and impactful life.

REFLECTIONS

Reflect on your current learning habits and how they align with your personal and professional goals. Are you actively seeking knowledge and wisdom, both spiritually and academically? Consider the areas in your life where you can invest more time and effort in learning. What specific steps can you take to prioritize continuous growth and education? Write down a plan that outlines how you will integrate learning into your daily routine, ensuring that you stay ahead in your field and enrich your life, just as Daniel and his friends did in their pursuit of knowledge.

30

Correct Your Mistakes

Don't forget to learn lessons from your mistakes.

> "By the rivers of Babylon, there we sat down, yea, we wept, when we remembered Zion."
>
> **Psalm 137:1**

The shrub forest of Babylon swayed gently in the wind, casting a somber shadow over our grieving hearts because we did not listen to the voice of your prophets (Dan 9:5-7). The sounds of the rushing river echoed our sorrow, a constant reminder of our captivity, shame, and yearning for the home we were forced to leave behind—our beloved land flowing with milk and honey (Ps 137). All of this happened because we ignored the warnings of God's prophets.

Our sins had expelled us from our homeland, leaving us to reminisce about Zion whenever we sat by the rivers of Babylon, longing to worship and sacrifice to the Lord our God in our sacred city (Dan 10:1-21). Now, our tears mingled with the flowing rivers of Babylon, as we have learned and understood that every word from God's mouth is righteous and true (Proverbs 8:8). We turn our faces to you, O Lord our God, seeking your mercy and forgiveness, confessing, *"O Lord, the great and awesome God, who keeps covenant and steadfast love with those who love him and keep his commandments"* (Daniel 9:3-4).

Mistakes are inevitable, and errors often stem from ignorance. It is crucial to learn from them, as they can serve as profound lessons (Dan 9:2-15). Acknowledging our mistakes and sins and taking responsibility for them can make us better individuals. Though sins may bring us down, but when we confess and repent, the Lord will forgive and lift us up again. The righteous rise again after falling seven times, whereas the wicked stumble in times of calamity (Proverbs 24:16).

Intentions matter, but they do not always guarantee positive outcomes. Even with good intentions, our actions can lead to unintended consequences. Reflecting on our intentions and being open to feedback are crucial steps toward learning from our mistakes. Ultimately, it is the impact of our actions that matters most, not just our intentions. Proverbs 14:12 warns that actions that seem right to us may lead to detrimental outcomes, proving the importance of humility and self-reflection. Recognising and admitting your mistakes is the first step toward right direction. Allowing us to avoid repeating the same errors and make wiser choices in the future.

However, merely acknowledging mistakes is not enough; we must actively reflect and take corrective action. Learning from our mistakes requires intentional effort to implement the lessons learned. Each mistake offers an opportunity for correction, growth, and refinement of our decisions and behaviours as we advance.

REFLECTIONS

Consider a recent mistake you made and the lessons it taught you. How did this experience shape your understanding of your actions and their consequences? Take time to think about what you could have done differently and how you can apply this knowledge moving forward. In your journal, write down the insights gained from this mistake and outline specific steps you can take to ensure growth and improvement in similar situations in the future. Embracing your past errors as opportunities for development can lead to a deeper relationship with God and a more intentional approach to your actions.

Further Reading and References

1 John 4:4; 1 Peter 2:9; 1 Samuel 2:9; 1 Samuel 8:5 1 Timothy 4:12, 16; 1 Timothy 4:15; 2 Corinthians 5:10; 2 Corinthians 7:6; 2 Corinthians 10:5; Amos 2:14-15; Deuteronomy 8:18; Ecclesiastes 2:14; Ecclesiastes 3:2; Ecclesiastes 11:9; Ephesians 5:14; Galatians 3:1; Galatians 6:7; Galatians 6:9; Genesis 11:4; Genesis 11:4; Genesis 27:40; Genesis 40:7; Genesis 40:7; Hebrews 2:16; Hebrews 11:6; Isaiah 40:21; Isaiah 43:2; Isaiah 47:10; Isaiah 59:1; Isaiah 60:1; James 1:6; James 1:27; James 3:13; Jeremiah 9:23; Jeremiah 33:3; Job 14:2; Job 14:5; Job 29:12; Job 32:13; John 4:12; John 14:12; Joshua 1:8; Luke 16:19; Luke 22:31; Matthew 4:6-7; Matthew 11:28; Matthew 16:13; Matthew 25:41; Philippians 4:8; Proverbs 21:25; Proverbs 22:29; Psalms 38:10; Psalms 127:1; Psalms 139:13; Revelation 3:18; Romans 12:2; Titus 3:9

Bibliography

Benner, David G. *The gift of being yourself: The sacred call to self-discovery.* InterVarsity Press, 2015.

Britannica, The Editors of Encyclopaedia. *"Mike Tyson"* Encyclopaedia Britannica, 7 May. 2024, https://www.britannica.com/biography/Mike-Tyson. Accessed 11 May 2024

Cadoux, Theodore John. *"Solon".* Encyclopedia Britannica, 9 Nov. 2023, https://www.britannica.com/biography/Solon. Accessed 1 March 2024

Chiru, Samson S., and Partakson Romun Chiru. *"The Irony of Little Drops of Water Makes the Mighty Ocean: The Economic Perspective in Manipur."* Politics Of Alternative Government: 219

Confessions, 1.1.1, Vernon J. Bourke, ed. Washington, DC; CUA Press, 1953

Dorothea Brande, *Wake Up & Live*, BN Publishing 2014

https://adfontesjournal.com/   Accessed

15/05/2024

Leadership Series by The World Leader Bishop David Oyedepo 2018

Norton, David, ed. *The New Cambridge Paragraph Bible with the Apocrypha*: King James Version. Revised edition. Cambridge, UK: Cambridge University Press, 2011. Print.

Russell Bertrand. *The conquest of happiness.* New York: Liveright. 1930

Spurgeon, Charles Haddon. *Spurgeon's Sermons.* Baker Book House, 1883

The Holy Bible: *English Standard Version.* Wheaton, IL: Crossway Bibles, 2016. Print.

The New International Version. Grand Rapids, MI: Zondervan, 2011. Print.

The New King James Version. Nashville: Thomas Nelson, 1982. Print.

The Holy Bible: King James Version. Electronic Edition of the 1900 Authorized Version. Bellingham, WA: Logos Research Systems, Inc., 2009. Print.

The Holy Bible: New Revised Standard Version.

Nashville: Thomas Nelson Publishers, 1989. Print.

Tyndale House Publishers. *Holy Bible: New Living Translation.* Carol Stream, IL: Tyndale House Publishers, 2015. Print.

Harris, W. Hall, III et al., eds. *The Lexham English Bible.* Bellingham, WA: Lexham Press, 2012. Print.

American Standard Version. Oak Harbor, WA: Logos Research Systems, Inc., 1995. Print.

https://www.biblegateway.com/ ERV

Author's Profile

Reverend Nana-Sei Tweretwie is a devoted servant of God with a rich legacy in ministry, spanning over three decades. As the Lead Pastor and Founder of Miracle Temple Assemblies of God in Milton Keynes, UK, he has planted and nurtured several congregations, including Miracle Temple Assemblies of God in Dichemso, a suburb of Kumasi, Ghana, and Bedford, UK and a co-planter of Grace Chapel Assemblies of God in Woking, UK. Currently on the groundwork for the Luton branch, His commitment to spreading the gospel extends beyond church walls, as he serves as a chaplaincy volunteer and plays a key role in missionary leadership across various global organisations.

With an apostolic mandate, Reverend Tweretwie has passionately pursued his calling for over 20 years, leveraging every opportunity to share the good news of Jesus Christ. With an MA in Biblical Studies and clear diligence, his global ministry has touched lives across continents, such as North America, Asia, Europe and Africa bringing salvation, healing, and revival countless individuals.

Reverend Tweretwie is married to Rev. Mrs Yvonne Tweretwie, and together, they are blessed with five children: Cecilia, Emmanuel, David, Samuel, and Joseph. The family is also blessed with three grandchildren namely Beatrice, Perpetual, and Foster. The Tweretwie family is deeply committed to the work of the Lord, actively participating in church and community activities, and inspiring others to live a life devoted to God.

Printed in Great Britain
by Amazon